HANNAH
THE HAIRY LITTLE MOOSE

Written by
Abdul Qader Ismail

Illustrated by
Amna Zaki

Copyright © 2025 Abdul Qader Ismail. All rights reserved. No part of this publication may be reproduced, distributed, or transmitted in any form or by any means without the prior written permission of the copyright holder, except by a reviewer who may quote brief passages in a review. For permission requests, contact ismail@abdulqader.org.

The story, all names, characters, and incidents portrayed in this production are fictitious. No identification with actual persons (living or deceased), places, buildings, and products is intended or should be inferred.

ISBN-13 (paperback): 978-1-0685857-5-3

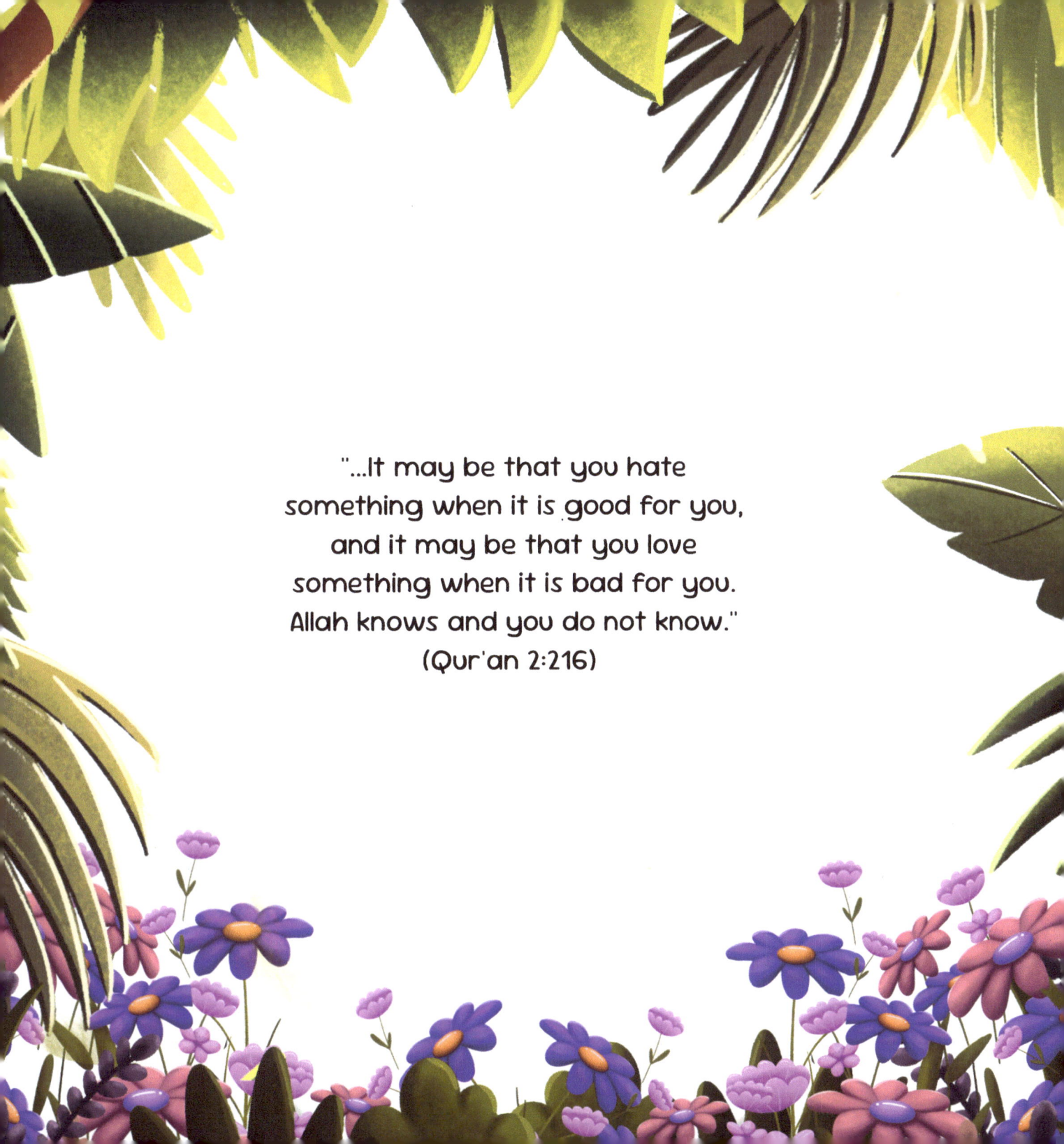

"...It may be that you hate something when it is good for you, and it may be that you love something when it is bad for you. Allah knows and you do not know."
(Qur'an 2:216)

Hannah, the hairy little moose, skipped happily through the woods. It was a beautiful summer's day. The Sun sat in the sky like a juicy orange. The trees whispered to their neighbours and the wind played hide-and-seek in their leaves.

Hannah was distracted.
She was scrunching her face up trying to get her tongue as far up her left nostril as she could.
She was fishing out a big, tasty bogey she had been saving up for the last few days.

WOOOSH! Suddenly a net sprang from the ground, leaves flying everywhere – a hunter's trap!

Caught in the trap was the rude chipmunk, furiously farting and wriggling his stubby little arms and legs from the holes in the net.

Hannah thought about how it was very nearly her stuck in the net instead!

Now, hurting her shin didn't seem so bad – in fact, she felt quite lucky.

Hannah sighed. Watching the chipmunk was fun but her Mama had always taught her to be kind to the other forest animals.
She nibbled through the net with her strong teeth, trying not to faint from the eggy smell of the chipmunk's yucky farts.
King Chickpoo dropped to the ground with a plop and scampered away.

Feeling hot, Hannah headed down to the river for a drink.
Along the way she stopped to smell some flowers. They were so bright and colourful, they looked good enough to eat!
She'd just started munching on a pink one when her mouth started buzzing angrily.

Opening her mouth, out flew a rather shocked and soggy bumblebee!
Hannah chased after the bee trying to talk to it.

Annoyed at this overgrown rat, the bee flew off to find another flower. But whichever flower the bee sat on, Hannah popped up next to it.

Seeing the river, Hannah remembered how thirsty she was and started slurping the delicious, cool water.

The cool water was helping soothe the pain, but it still hurt! Hannah was feeling very sorry for herself when she spotted a dark shape moving in the trees.

The wolf looked this way and that, sniffing the air before slinking back into the trees.

Hannah's lungs felt like they were going to burst, but she made herself wait until she was sure the wolf was gone.
'YHAAahh!' She gasped as she surfaced and took a deep breath.

Forgetting about her sore bum, Hannah thought about how close she had come to being dinner for the wolf.
The bee sting had saved her life!

Feeling quite grateful, Hannah climbed out of the water and shook herself dry.
Catching her reflection in the water, she looked like a giant furball with googly eyes.
As she stood on the riverbank making funny faces at herself, Hannah suddenly realised the Sun was getting ready for bed!

Trotting home, Hannah spotted a shortcut. Her Baba had warned her about this part of the forest, but she was already late for dinner. She decided to take it!

The Moon was coming out to play and Hannah shivered as she felt its cool breath. She started to walk faster, feeling a bit scared.
The trees crowded around her, their branches reaching down like long claws.
It was dark and smelly. Perhaps all the mean, scary creatures of the forest lived here.

In her hurry to get home, Hannah didn't notice the ground was starting to feel soggy.
With each step, her little hooves were sinking into thick, gloopy mud.
Hannah had walked right into a swamp!

But out from under the leaves scampered a chubby little chipmunk – King Chickpoo the Third! And from all around her emerged a whole tribe of furry little balls.
Hannah breathed a sigh of relief.

King Chickpoo scampered onto her head. He squeaked some orders, and the chipmunks of the Hairy Nutter Clan started pulling Hannah out of the swamp. Each chipmunk was light enough not to sink into the mud but working together they were strong enough to pull her out.

The chipmunks vanished back into the forest.
Hannah tried to thank King Chickpoo in her best chipmunk.

When they arrived home, King Chickpoo had a chat with Baba moose while Hannah washed her hair and ate dinner.

Afterwards, she snuggled with her Baba and told him all about her adventures.

"Do you know King Chickpoo?" Hannah asked, yawning.

"Everyone knows King Chickpoo," her Baba replied, "He's a very important chipmunk. Now, go to sleep my little mushroom."

"Do you know King Chickpoo?"

"Everyone knows King Chickpoo"

When she was with her Baba, Hannah felt safe. Baba moose could crush mountains under his hooves and hold up the sky with his antlers. He had a tickly beard, bushy eyebrows, and hairy nostrils. No-one messed with Hannah's Baba, not even the big brown bears!

She snuggled deeper into her Baba's thick, warm hair. Just as she was falling off to sleep, Hannah finally managed to get the juicy bogey out of her left nostril.

The Mighty Moose!

- Moose are the largest members of the deer family.
- Moose have thick, dark brown fur and prefer cold weather.
- Moose live in the northern parts of North America, Europe and Asia.
- Moose's wide hooves help them walk on snow.
- A full-grown adult moose can be 7 feet tall and as heavy as a car.
- Male moose grow antlers each year, and they can grow up to 6 feet across.
- Moose can run at up to 35 miles per hour.
- The front legs of a moose are longer than their back legs, which helps them jump over things.
- Moose are herbivores (plant eaters).
- Moose like to swim; they can stay underwater for 30 seconds.
- A male moose is called a bull, a female moose a cow, and a baby moose a calf.
- The plural for moose is moose (not meese, or mice!).

www.ingramcontent.com/pod-product-compliance
Lightning Source LLC
Chambersburg PA
CBHW041536040426
42446CB00002B/112